essentials

Getting Published

Time-saving books that teach specific skills to busy people, focusing on what really matters; the things that make a difference – the *essentials*.

Other books in the series include:

Going for Self-employment

Making the Bridegroom's Speech

Writing Great Copy

Making the Most of Your Time

Remembering Names and Faces

Writing Successful Essays

Feeling Good for No Good Reason

Pass Your Practical Driving Test

Responding to Stress

Getting Published

Chriss McCallum

Published in 2001 by
How To Books Ltd, 3 Newtec Place,
Magdalen Road, Oxford OX4 1RE, United Kingdom
Tel: (01865) 793806   Fax: (01865) 248780
email: info@howtobooks.co.uk
www.howtobooks.co.uk

British Library Cataloguing in Publication Data
A catalogue record for this book is available from
the British Library

Edited by Francesca Mitchell
Cover design by Shireen Nathoo Design, London
Produced for How To Books by Deer Park Productions
Designed and typeset by Shireen Nathoo Design, London
Printed and bound in Great Britain

NOTE: The material contained in this book is set out in good faith for
general guidance and no liability can be accepted for loss or expense
incurred as a result of relying in particular circumstances on statements
made in the book. The laws and regulations are complex and liable to
change, and readers should check the current position with the relevant
authorities before making personal arrangements.

ESSENTIALS *is an imprint of*
How To Books

Contents

Preface

'The only sensible ends of literature are, first, the pleasurable toil of writing; second, the gratification of one's family and friends; and, lastly, the solid cash.' *(Nathaniel Hawthorne)*

Let's begin by blowing away a great big myth: publishing is *not* a closed shop. You don't have to 'know someone'.

Publishers need writers. Without writers there would be nothing for them to publish. If *you* can offer quality work to the right market at the right time, you'll have as good a chance of success as anyone.

What does it take, then, to be a published writer? Well, you have to be able to put your thoughts and ideas into words that others will understand. You write to communicate. It's equally important, though, to know how to *sell* what you write.

You're stepping into a fiercely competitive business and the odds against you could be high, especially if you're writing fiction or poetry. However, you can do a lot to reduce those odds. You can get ahead of all those writers who send their work out without any clear marketing strategy.

The writers who get their work published are not necessarily the most brilliant. They are writers who provide what editors and publishers want.

Being a successful writer means balancing your individuality and enthusiasm with your writing and selling skills. It means

~ adopting a professional attitude from the start

~ writing as well as you can in your chosen field

~ giving editors what they want, not what you think they should want

~ presenting your work as editors like to see it

~ developing a mutually profitable relationship with editors.

This book will help you get published. It defines the things that really matter about finding and approaching the best markets for your work. It shows you how to achieve your goal and see your name in print.

Chriss McCallum

1 Preparing to be a Published Writer

'Luck is what happens when preparation meets opportunity.'
(Jack Valenti)

In this chapter, six things that really matter:

~ **Being professional**
~ **Balancing your enthusiasm with the needs of the market**
~ **Understanding your rights – and other people's**
~ **Finding the right market**
~ **Preparing your manuscript**
~ **Approaching the market**

The world is full of would-be writers. Most of them are wasting not only their own time but also the time of the editors and publishers they bombard with unsuitable short stories, novels, poetry, articles and books. Their work is rejected time after time, not necessarily because they can't write, but because they don't know how to market their work effectively.

This is sad for them but fortunate for you, because it means there's less competition for writers who study the market, supply the right material when and where it's wanted, and go about the business of selling in a professional way. *You* can be one of those successful writers.

There are markets for almost anything you want to write. You'll learn how to find them, analyse them, approach them, and sell to them.

Is this you?

I send short stories and poems to every magazine I can think of but keep getting rejections. • Why don't the editors who reject my work tell me what's wrong with it? • Why shouldn't I save money (and trees) by typing in single spacing? • I've written a novel but haven't a clue where to send it. • I'm worried in case my ideas get stolen. • I'd like an agent but don't know how to get one. • I don't know anyone in publishing – how can I meet the right people?

Being professional

Starting now, think of yourself as a professional. A professional attitude gives you a huge and immediate advantage over 99% of writers who are trying to break into the market.

First impressions count, and editors respond favourably to

~ courteous, concise, businesslike letters

~ brief businesslike email or telephone queries

~ queries and submissions that show familiarity with their publication or publishing list

~ submissions addressed correctly by name to the appropriate person

~ manuscripts (mss, singular ms) presented in standard format (see pages 95 and 96)

~ self-addressed reply envelopes (s.a.e.) bearing adequate return postage.

Editors don't like

~ submissions of material that has no relevance to their needs

~ rambling, chatty emails or phone calls

~ uninvited faxes blocking urgent incoming material

~ letters on pages torn from lined notebooks or jotters

~ manuscripts typed in single or one-and-a-half-line spacing, in faint print, in fancy typefaces, on a worn-out ribbon, on thin paper

~ dog-eared, much-corrected, coffee-stained manuscripts

~ tatty recycled s.a.e.s which they're expected to seal with sticky tape *

~ even worse, no s.a.e.

Sending a tatty submission is like turning up for an interview in crumpled clothes. It does not inspire confidence.

Editors are busy people. They don't have time to write critiques of your work, and that isn't their job anyway. Their job is to find publishable material to fill their magazine or their book list. *

The writing is *your* business. It's *your* job to study their magazine or the kind of books they publish, and offer them the best you can produce that might, at the very least, be suitable for their needs. You waste everybody's time, including your own, if you send inappropriate material.

Don't, on the other hand, offer a clone of something they've just published. Editors look for fresh and original work, not a rehash of last week's article or a clone of the latest bestseller.

Balancing your enthusiasm with the needs of the market

Keep a clear picture of your target market in your mind while you write. Every magazine and every publishing house has its own style, flavour and ethos. Writers who don't (or won't) understand this get it wrong far more often than they get it right, condemning themselves to frustration and rejection slips.

* Editors are not writing tutors. Don't ask (or expect) them to coach you in the craft of writing.

The trick is, to write for the market but retain your own 'voice' and your enthusiasm for your subject. *

Too much tinkering and tailoring to the market could polish the heart out of your writing. Aim to produce work written with zest in your natural voice, and which is right for its target market. It's a delicate balance.

Understanding your rights – and other people's

You don't need to register copyright in the UK. (In the USA, registration is standard practice.) Copyright belongs to you the minute you put your words on paper or screen, and the law protects your copyright during your lifetime and for 70 years after your death.

You can give away or sell the copyright in any of your work if you wish, but you might live to rue the day. Copyright is a property, potentially as valuable as a winning lottery ticket. Your short story might inspire a TV

A contrived style seldom works, and certainly won't fool an editor.

series, your novel be optioned for a film, your character become as lucrative as Ian Fleming's James Bond. If you no longer own the copyright, you can't claim any of the profits. The publishing world is full stories of fortunes lost in this way. *

And if you're worried about your work being stolen – unlikely, but you might feel the need for reassurance – send a copy of the manuscript to yourself by registered post, then deposit the unopened package with a bank or solicitor and get a dated receipt.

Be careful about quoting from other people's writing. You can't quote more than a line or two of someone else's work without permission, other than in 'fair dealing' (imprecisely defined as 'the legitimate use of work in quotation for purposes of criticism or review provided due acknowledgement is given').

There's no copyright in facts or ideas, but if you use someone else's storyline to a recognisable extent you might be accused of plagiarism.

The von Trapp family of The Sound of Music fame sold all their rights the day they arrived in America, for the price of a few nights' lodging; they never saw a cent of the millions of dollars made from their story.

The Society of Authors publishes a series of Quick Guides, including a guide to copyright. These are free to members, and available to non-members at modest prices from £1.00 to around £5.00. For a full list of current Quick Guides and prices write, enclosing an s.a.e., to The Society of Authors, 84 Drayton Gardens, London SW10 9SB.

Finding the right market

The two main writers' directories will give you leads to appropriate magazines and publishing houses. These are *The Writers' & Artists' Yearbook* (A & C Black) and *The Writer's Handbook* (Macmillan). Both are updated annually, and should be in your local library. Make sure you see the latest edition.

Look, too, at *The Small Press Guide* and *The Guide to Book Publishers*, published annually by Writers' Bookshop, Remus House, Coltsfoot Drive, Peterborough PE2 9JX.

Some UK and nearly all US magazines and publishing houses offer writers' guidelines. These save time and work for both writers and editors, so do send for them if they're available. *

More and more magazines and publishing houses are posting guidelines on the Internet. You can usually print these out or copy and paste them into your computer's word-processing program.

The most common complaint editors make about writers is, 'They don't bother to find out what we publish.' Don't give any editor cause to say that about you.

Writers need contacts. That doesn't mean you have to be related to the editor-in-chief or married to the company accountant. It does mean mixing with other writers and meeting editors and agents. So get out there and network: go to writers' conferences, the bigger the better; take a writers' holiday. Most writers' gatherings are informal; everyone talks to everyone else, from raw beginner to best-selling author. The writing community is a friendly zone; you could find yourself queueing for tea between an agent

Guidelines are helpful, but they're no substitute for thorough study of the publication itself.

and an editor and chatting with both. Don't make a nuisance of yourself, though. If you want an editor or agent to look at your work, send it to their office; you won't be popular if you thrust an uninvited manuscript into their hands. *

Preparing your manuscript

One of the biggest days in your life as a writer is the day you put your first submission into the post. Here's how to present your work like a professional:

~ Check your facts. Even a tiny factual error will make an editor wonder if you've made a serious slip somewhere.

~ Check that your text is clear, concise, correct and complete.

~ Check your spelling. Don't rely on a computer spell-check; it won't recognise correctly spelled words wrongly used, like 'their' instead of 'there'. Use a dictionary.

~ Check your grammar and syntax. Make

It won't do any harm, when you write, to remind the editor or agent that you met them at this or that event.

sure your meaning is clear and unambiguous.

~ Proofread your work meticulously. When you've read a page, read it again from the bottom line up; this helps reveal mistakes you might have missed in a conventional read-through.

~ Make your manuscript look as good as you can. *

Prose, which includes short stories, novels, articles and non-fiction books, should be double spaced (one *full* line of space between lines of type) in plain black 12 point roman type on one side only of plain white A4 paper. Don't justify (make even) the right-hand edge.

Leave good margins all round, at least a full inch (2.5 cm). These are needed for marking editorial and typesetting instructions. See the example on page 95.

Number the sheets consecutively throughout, starting with '1' on the first page of text and running straight through to the

* You only get one chance to make a first impression – don't blow it.

end. (*Don't* start at '1' again for each new chapter.) The pages can then be kept in order, even if they slip off the desk in a heap. It does happen, even in the best-run offices. At the bottom right of every page except the last, type 'mf', meaning 'more follows'. After the last line of type on the last page, type 'ends'.

Don't bind your manuscript or tie it with fancy ribbons or decorate it with pictures. *

Never use staples. Paperclip a short ms, put a longer ms in a document file, and a full length book ms in a typing-paper box or secured in rubber bands.

Use medium-weight, 80 or 90 gsm (grams per square metre) white A4 paper. Buy your paper and envelopes from an office supplier; they offer better value than the high street.

Poetry should be presented in plain black 12 or 14 point roman type, *one poem only to each A4 sheet*, stanzas single-spaced, with your name and address on every sheet. See the example on page 96.

You need adequate equipment, at least an

* Ask any editor or judge and they'll tell you that, invariably, the fancier the package the worse the writing.

electronic typewriter or a decent word processor with a good printer. Handwritten manuscripts will not be read anywhere nowadays (other than for 'Letters to the Editor'). Invest in a computer and an inkjet or laser printer if you can afford them.

Many magazines now want text that's sharp and clear enough to be scanned into a computer, and it's no longer unusual for magazine editors and book publishers to demand material on computer disk. If you can't supply your work in the required format, you could lose sales.

Approaching the market

Your approach will depend on the kind of work you want to place. Some magazines specify their preferred approach either in the publication itself, or in their guidelines, or in the reference books mentioned on page 16. Otherwise, be guided by these conventions:

~ Short stories – send the complete manuscript with a brief covering letter.

~ Novels – send a covering letter, a synopsis and the first two or three chapters (not more than about 50 pages) as a sample. We'll look at agents, and what they can do for you, in Chapter 3.

~ Poetry – send four to six poems at a time.

~ Articles – send a query letter and outline. Send humorous pieces in full, though; humour can't be explained or outlined.

~ Non-fiction books – send a cover letter, a synopsis, a chapter-by-chapter outline, and sample chapters.

Whatever you're sending, always enclose a suitable s.a.e.

Do enclose a covering letter. This serves to offer a 'handshake' to the editor. A courteous businesslike letter and a crisp, correction-free manuscript in standard format will inspire confidence in your professionalism, and show that you take a serious attitude to your work. You want the editor to know you're a writer he or she can do business with. *

* Your letter is also useful for sending on to the accounts department so they have all your details handy when it's time to pay you.

Whatever the editor's decision, accept it with grace. Rejection is part of every writer's life. If your work is turned down, there are probably good reasons. You might not be told what these are, but *don't* pester the editor for explanations. You don't want to be labelled 'nuisance'.

There are markets for children's stories, novels, non-fiction articles and books, which are as varied as adult markets. Find and study some of the excellent books available on writing for children, and apply the same marketing principles. *

Caution: reputable publishers do not advertise for manuscripts.

You've probably seen advertisements in the press, inviting writers to send manuscripts: 'Does your book deserve publication' and so on.

Be wary: doing business with these firms could cost you dearly, both in money and reputation. The writers' reference books (page 16) explain how these companies work and the risks involved.

* Writing for children, like bringing them up, requires a special touch. Don't make the mistake of thinking it's easier than writing for adults – it isn't.

Summary points

★ Be professional in every aspect of your writing and the business of selling it.

★ Balance your instinctive enthusiasm for your writing with the requirements of the market you want to write for.

★ Understand your rights, and respect the rights of others.

★ Find the right market for your work by studying all the information available.

★ Prepare your work in the appropriate standard format.

★ Approach the market with courtesy and respect the editor's decision.

2 Getting your Short Story Published

'Something that can be read in an hour and remembered for a lifetime.'   *(Stephen Vincent Benét)*

In this chapter, six things that really matter:

~ **Assessing the market**
~ **Writing for consumer magazines**
~ **Getting started with the small press**
~ **Marketing your short story**
~ **Entering short story competitions**
~ **Building a collection**

These are buoyant times for the short story. Several well-established women's magazines now produce regular spin-off titles devoted to short fiction. These are proving to be good sellers. They offer writers substantial payment for the right kind of stories – stories that will make their readers eager to buy the next issue … and the next.

Although the target readership is mainly female, both sexes are welcome to write for these magazines. They publish a wide variety of stories including mysteries, romances, family tales, ghost stories, 'spine-chillers', twist-enders.

There are short fiction slots in many weekly and monthly magazines, including some hobby titles.

The independent press, too, is flourishing, and there are dozens of short story competitions every year; these are the places to try those quirky off-beat stories the mainstream magazines don't want.

Thorough study of the market is your key to success. Remember you're a salesperson as well as a writer. Target your markets with care and your acceptance rate will soar.

Is this you?

I send my short stories to every magazine I can think of, but have nothing but rejections to show for my efforts. • I don't want to write romantic stories, but that's all that seems to get published. • I spend a fortune entering competitions but never even get placed. • I really want to write a novel, but I've been advised to try short stories first, as they're easier. • I sent a dozen of my short stories to some book publishers but they don't seem to be interested.

Assessing the market

Whatever kind of short story you write, you're creating a product which you hope to sell. Don't be precious about this. To market your short story successfully, you need to target the right outlet. *

You'll be wasting your own and everyone else's time if you offer, say, a horror story to *The Lady* or a teenage romance to *Hello!* You might find it hard to believe, but there are writers out there who do daft things like that.

To some degree, success can be down to luck. You might work long and hard, you

* As George Bernard Shaw said, 'Literature is like any other trade; you'll never sell anything unless you go to the right shop.'

might even know the editor's auntie, but what ultimately matters is the words you put on the page and whether somebody likes them enough to want them at that particular time.

Give Lady Luck a helping hand: offer your stories only to magazines that publish the kind of story you write, and your chances will be countless times greater than those of the legions of writers who don't bother with market research.

Don't imagine that short stories are easier to write just because they're short. It takes real discipline and powerful writing to create a successful story in a limited amount of words. Every word must count, must justify its inclusion. *

Experienced writers will tell you that it's actually easier to write a novel, provided you have enough stamina.

In the short story, emotion rules. In today's popular short-short stories in particular, emotion is compressed and intensified

* Every word must earn its place. Be ruthless: discard anything that doesn't need to be there.

through economy of words.

Study the craft of writing short stories. There are plenty of books around to help you. Ask at your library, look on the 'Creative Writing' shelves in the bookshops. Work at it, and you'll succeed.

Writing for consumer magazines

Take no notice of writers who say there's no market for short stories. These are almost always writers who don't bother with market research or who just don't write well enough to be published.

The popular magazines can't get enough good stories; editors sometimes have to send out SOS messages to writers they know to be reliable, asking for 'a 750-word twister' or 'a 1,000-word mystery – by Friday, please!' Build a reputation for 'delivering the goods' and you could find yourself on the receiving end of calls like that.

Editors love to receive well written, entertaining, *publishable* short stories, but complain that most of the stories cluttering up their desks are dull, clichéd, lifeless, formless, sad or despairing, with hackneyed plots and cardboard characters. Editors need stories that will please their readers. Give them what they want, and they'll welcome you with open cheque-books.

Search for possible markets at independent newsagents as well as the big chains. The main high-street outlets stock only what they know will sell in quantity. Independents can make more individual and adventurous choices.

Look at hobby magazines – they sometimes publish fiction relevant to their subject. Scour the reference books, too, for leads. Spend time selecting three or four magazines you believe your story would suit. *

Never use out-of-date issues for research. It's vital to know what your target magazine is publishing *today*, not what they published a year or even a couple of months ago.

Before you go any further, you need to make sure the magazines you're interested in will at least consider your submission. Many

* Many a good story is rejected simply because it's been sent to the wrong market.

magazines, including some of the big-selling glossies, won't look at unsolicited work; they might tell you so in their masthead (the column giving information about the magazine, its staff, advertising, parentage and so on). This is a defence against floods of irrelevant time-wasting material. Leave these markets alone at this stage. Try them later when you've achieved a few successes and can send them clips of your published work.

Buy three or four consecutive issues of your target magazines and read them from cover to cover, including the adverts. *

Advertisers spend their money shrewdly; they target exactly the people their products will appeal to. Build a picture of each magazine's typical reader. Can you empathise with this person? Would they like the kind of story you've written or want to write?

Checklist for short stories:

* Keep the receipts – this is an expense you can set against tax.

~ Are your main characters in the same age group as this magazine's typical reader?

~ Could this reader identify with these characters?

~ Does your story *look* easy to read, with plenty of dialogue and not too many solid paragraphs?

~ Does the story start with a strong 'hook', setting up dramatic tension in the first paragraph?

~ And does it end with a satisfying and *believable* 'feel-good' conclusion?

~ Is the viewpoint clear and consistent?

~ Is the language appropriate to your target publication?

~ Does the writing appeal to the five senses?

~ Do your characters develop and change as a result of the story's action?

Mainstream magazines generally like upbeat endings that leave their readers feeling good and waiting eagerly for the next issue. Keep downbeat stories for competitions and literary magazines.

If your target magazines offer writers'

guidelines, send for them. Many magazines regard as taboo subjects like abortion, suicide, rape, drugs, AIDS, child abuse, horror and science fiction; some dislike first person narrative. Studying the magazines should give you a sound idea of what they do like, but guidelines can be helpful. Don't be tempted to rely on them as a substitute for actual market study, though. *

Getting started with the small press

Our independent presses, universally called the small press, are the lifeblood of innovative short fiction. Almost invariably, their publications are produced on a minimal budget by a single enthusiast or a small team working in their spare time and relying on reciprocal advertising for publicity.

Independent magazines don't have to please a corporate boardroom, profit-seeking shareholders or big-money advertisers. They can publish what they like – and what they like is imaginative, cutting-edge prose and poetry, the kind of work which has little

* *There is absolutely no substitute for hands-on study of your target magazine.*

chance of finding a home in the commercial mainstream. This is where you're most likely to place that lovingly crafted but non-commercial story. You're also much more likely to get some feedback on your story from a small-press editor, although you shouldn't ask for or expect this. *

Many writers who achieve mainstream success carry on writing for their favourite small press magazines. They like the freedom to write on subjects and in styles that don't fit the constraints of the commercial world.

Some small-press magazines carry considerable clout, and some of the better-produced titles are sold in major bookshops. Though most pay very little, some improve their rates as they become more successful. You shouldn't regard the small press as merely a jumping-off point to bigger markets, although without doubt they've given many a now-famous writer an encouraging start.

When you've found one or two magazines you like, take out a subscription. It's to our

* *Remember that any feedback you get is only the opinion of one person. Another editor might take a different view.*

mutual advantage for writers to support the small press.

Marketing your short story

You've analysed your target market, and you're ready to send your baby out into the world. Here's how to do it:

~ Address your envelope and covering letter to the fiction editor by name. If the name isn't given in the masthead, phone the switchboard and ask; make sure you get the spelling right. *

~ Keep your covering letter brief, giving your name, address and phone number or email address, and writing on the lines of 'Dear Maude Pinkpen, Please consider the enclosed short story "The Last Rose" (1,550 words) for publication at your usual rates. Yours sincerely, Gemma Trying-Hard.'

~ Enclose your ms, typed in standard format.

~ Enclose a suitably sized and stamped s.a.e.

* Editors move about a lot. You won't help your cause by writing to an editor who left a couple of issues ago.

And that's it … short, simple and businesslike. Don't explain your story, and don't tell the editor how brilliant your writing tutor, your writers' circle and your mother think it is.

Don't send more than one story at a time, and don't send the same story to more than one magazine at the same time.

Entering short story competitions

There are plenty of short story competitions around, some offering substantial prizes. Look for them in both mainstream and small-press magazines and get your name on mailing lists. Magazines like *The Lady* and *Good Housekeeping* run them regularly and offer publication as part of the prize – what a boost to your writing career, to be published in a national magazine.

Take care, though, to avoid any competition that requires you to relinquish copyright in your story – you could be signing away a fortune. *

* Hold on to your copyright – that story might keep you in your old age.

Your storyline might inspire a TV series or a film, and not a penny would be yours. You would also have written off any overseas sales you might have made for yourself in the many lucrative markets in the English-speaking world, as well as foreign language sales.

Here's a statistic that might shock you: on average, 85% of entries to short story competitions fail at the first reading. Given that fact, how can you make sure *your* story survives that first cull? Read on ...

What do you think is uppermost in a judge's mind when he or she sits down to read those hundreds, maybe thousands, of entries? Finding a great story? Discovering an exciting new writer? Well, maybe ... but the hard truth is this: in the first sift, the judge will be mainly concerned with getting that pile down to a manageable number. Every manuscript that can legitimately be eliminated will be. Believe me – I've done it. *

* Don't give the judge any reason to eliminate your entry on a technicality.

Here's how to make sure your story stays in the running:

~ Read the rules and read them again; read them thoroughly, and follow them to the letter.

~ Write what is asked for. A short story is a piece of prose fiction. Articles, essays, personal experiences and narrative poems won't qualify; nor will children's stories unless they're specified as eligible.

~ Respect the stipulated length absolutely.

~ Present your story in standard manuscript layout (see page 95).

~ Avoid done-to-death plots: the old lady who walks through a wall; the prize roses growing above the buried corpse; the lonely-hearts story where the husband or wife turns up as the 'date'; the disguised narrator (surprise, surprise, I'm a cat! – or a dog, or a frog, or a ghost – or a vampire or an alien); the wife thinking her husband is having an affair then finding he's been planning a surprise for her; and the biggest groan-raiser of all, '… and then I woke up – it had all been a terrible dream'.

Every judge has seen all these too many times already.

Building a collection

No book publisher is going to be interested in a collection of your short stories unless your name is well known – not necessarily as a writer – or you've already had an impressive number of stories published in reasonably well-known magazines and/or you've won some prestigious competitions. *

So be patient. Wait till you have enough stories in print to put together a collection of the best of these plus a few new original stories. That's the time to send out feelers to publishers.

Summary points

* Collections by unknown writers simply don't sell, so publishers won't take a chance on them.

★ Assess the market carefully before you submit either a query letter or a full manuscript. Don't submit work to a magazine you've never read.

★ Write for the high-paying consumer magazines. You'll build future success by being able to send prestigious clips.

★ Get started with the small press. They might not pay much (if anything), but a published story is a published story and shows that an editor has thought it good enough to accept.

★ Market your story effectively, selecting the most probable targets.

★ Enter short story competitions – they offer more freedom in the type of story you can enter.

★ Build a track record of published stories before you put a collection together.

3 Getting Your Novel Published

'A novelist is in the entertainment business. Your job is to tell a story others will find interesting.' (Tom Clancy)

In this chapter, six things that really matter:

- ~ **Writing a saleable novel**
- ~ **Revising and rewriting**
- ~ **Preparing a submission package**
- ~ **Finding and approaching an agent**
- ~ **Offering your novel directly to publishers**
- ~ **Helping to sell your novel**

Put aside thoughts of the Booker or the Whitbread, and aim to produce a novel that is both interesting and entertaining. Agents and publishers look for a story that will grip readers *from the opening paragraphs*, keep them turning the pages and leave them impatient for your next one.

The odds are heavily stacked against the

first-time novelist, with only one in 2000 submitted manuscripts achieving publication. That figure hasn't changed for 50 years, and certainly isn't rising.

Most publishing houses nowadays are accountant- rather than editor-led, so unless the finance people see your novel as a potential money-maker, it won't stand a chance.

To succeed, then, your novel must shine like a diamond among the dross.

Is this you?

I've written a novel but I don't know where to send my manuscript. • I've sent my novel to several publishers but they've sent it straight back. • I've been advised to get an agent but don't know how. What could an agent do for me anyway? • I've just read a novel that seems to be selling by the truckload – I'm sure I could write one just like it. • I'm wondering if I should publish my novel on the Internet.

Writing a saleable novel

Is your idea commercial? Will it sell? Nobody really knows. Novels by unknown writers can take off and make millions. Novels by 'bankable' writers can flop. Nobody has yet managed to bottle 'Essence of Bestseller'.

So what persuades someone to buy a novel? The author's name? The cover? The blurb on the back cover? The first page? Reviews? All or any of these, perhaps.

As your name is not yet famous, neither you, your agent nor your publisher will know if your novel is a success till it's out there in the shops and people are buying it – or not.

What kind of novel are you writing? Will it appeal to a wide readership, or does it fall into a specific category? *

You need to know this, so you can approach the agents or publishers most likely to be interested.

'General' fiction covers almost any novel that can't be categorised. This is where you'll find writers like Margaret Atwood, Patrick O'Brian and Wilbur Smith.

* *You need to know the market you're aiming for. You can't afford to rely on luck.*

Most general novels are 70,000 to 100,000 words in length, though there are many exceptions.

'Genre' fiction, sometimes called 'category' fiction, is fiction that can be pigeon-holed as 'crime', 'romance', 'adventure', 'Western' and so on. Most genre novels are between 50,000 and 75,000 words.

'Literary' or 'experimental' fiction recognises no limits, so can't be pinned down; it's the hardest kind of fiction to place.

Wherever your novel might fit, look at market trends. Why spend months, maybe years, writing something the trade knows won't sell? Most weekend newspapers print Bestseller lists which will give you a guide to what is currently popular.

Don't jump on a bandwagon, though. It might take two or three years to write and place your novel, see it through the publishing process and into the shops. The wagon you've hitched your hopes to could be sinking to the bottom of a ditch by then.

Be true to yourself. Write the novel you want to write, and make it as good as you possibly can. *

You must hook the publisher's reader in the first five pages or you've lost him.

Check your novel for saleability:

~ Do you have a powerful lead character – a courageous hero, a spirited heroine, strong enough to make your readers care about them, identify with them, and remember them for years? (Think Scarlett O'Hara, James Bond, Harry Potter) *

~ Does your main character have a compelling motivation, a driving ambition, a 'high-stakes' goal?

~ Does your central character grow and develop in the course of the story?

~ Does your hero or heroine have real opposition, a strong adversary?

~ Have you created fully rounded characters who 'live and breathe', people your readers will believe in?

~ Have you set your story in a world which readers will find attractive? People enjoy novels that take them into worlds beyond their own experience, worlds they'll only ever know through stories. Art, antiques,

* People remember characters far more vividly than they remember plots.

theatre, film, TV, sport, music, fashion, finance, international politics, law, police and detection – backgrounds and professions like these will lend glamour to your story and captivate your readers. Dentistry or road-mending, for example, probably won't. *

~ Is there plenty of conflict and action, without it being too complicated? An over-complex plot might confuse readers and lead to loose ends being left untied.

~ Is your story well-paced, with no flagging patches?

~ Have you created a powerful ending, with your main character coming through a major problem, either physical or emotional?

~ Does your ending satisfy the expectations you've set up?

No-one exists in a vacuum. Your characters must inhabit some kind of believable world.

A caution: Think carefully before you include contemporary references such as political figures, personalities, current events and so on. While they might lend immediacy to your story, they will 'date' your book, fixing the story at a particular moment in time and possibly reducing the chances of building up a 'timeless' and saleable backlist. Your novel might even be out of date before it gets published because of the time it takes to get a book through the publishing process.

Revising and rewriting

Whether you write it straight through in a white heat, or chapter by chapter revising as you go, your novel should be revised, rewritten, and polished before submission. *

Look at your work with a cold eye, checking that:

~ the structure is sound

~ the storyline is logical and believable; you haven't relied on coincidence to explain events, or included anything that might cause the reader to ask 'Would they *really*?'

~ your grammar is correct and your syntax

* Don't be so pleased with your first draft that you think it can't be improved. That's a fast route to rejection.

makes sense; you've actually said what you meant to say

~ your spelling is impeccable; don't rely on spell checkers, they can't pick up correctly spelled words wrongly used, like shear/sheer

~ you haven't repeated favourite or striking words and/or phrases.

Preparing a submission package

Whether you choose to approach an agent first or offer your novel directly to a publisher, you need to prepare a submission package. Agents and editors want to be able to assess your novel in a concise, easily digested form. *

You need:

~ a covering letter with a *short* précis of your story, addressed to the editor or agent *by name*; if appropriate, you could mention that your story would appeal to readers who enjoy a particular well-known author;

* It's unprofessional to send a complete manuscript before you're asked to do so.

be concise and businesslike; *do not* offer your own, your best friend's or your writing group's opinion of your novel – this is unprofessional and counter-productive

~ biographies of your main characters: two or three paragraphs per character outlining key personal traits and showing them as fully rounded and having the potential to make readers care about them

~ a synopsis of the whole novel, written in the present tense, touching on all the key scenes, and showing: whose story it is, what your main character wants, what lies between them and their goal, how they achieve that goal

~ the *first* two or three chapters – no more than 50 pages or so – to demonstrate your story-telling talent and writing ability

~ your author biography, including anything that makes you interesting and saleable as an author

~ adequate return postage.

Finding and approaching an agent

Publishers will look at your novel a lot more quickly and favourably if they receive it from an agent. However, it's far from easy to find an agent if you're a first-time novelist. *

Agents are choosy, which is understandable because they make no money till their authors do. The agent bears the expense of contacting editors, sending out copies of your manuscript, arranging auctions etc., but earns nothing till you sign a contract and bank an advance against royalties.

Basically, the agent's job is to

~ find the right publisher for your novel

~ negotiate contracts and secure the best possible deal

~ look after your various rights and exploit them to the full

~ check your royalty statements and make sure you get paid.

In return, the agent takes an agreed

An agent will only take you on if they're totally confident they can place your novel.

percentage of your income.

An agent won't write your novel for you, though they might offer editorial advice.

Ask your published writer friends to recommend a good agency. Or ask the Society of Authors (page 16) for information from their most recent survey – they keep a list of agents recommended by their members.

There is also an Association of Authors' Agents, identified in the yearbooks by an asterisk. This is the trade association of British agents, and members are committed to a code of practice.

Offer your novel to only one agent at a time. Never send a full manuscript. Most agents indicate in the reference books their preferred method of approach. Respect this. If they're interested, they'll ask to see the full manuscript for further assessment.

Agents look for writers who are likely to have more than one novel in them. While you're trying to place your first novel, make a start on your next one, perhaps getting a draft outline down on paper. It's usual nowadays for a publisher to offer a two-book deal; a second book in the pipeline could help the agent clinch that deal for you.

Don't expect a response overnight, but if you hear nothing for a month, chase them up *courteously*.

When an agency takes you on, they might suggest revisions or ask for rewrites. Trust them – they know what editors want. It's vital that you and your agent develop a mutually supportive and profitable relationship; you can only do this by working as a team.

Offering your novel directly to publishers

If you can't interest an agent, try offering your novel directly to publishers. Search out those who publish your kind of novel: look in the writers' reference books, in bookshops and publishers' catalogues. *

* Call the publicity department for a catalogue, or read it on the publisher's website.

Discount any publisher who only looks at manuscripts submitted by agents.

It's usual to approach publishers one at a

time, but if you're in a hurry and can afford the expense, you could send out multiple submissions. This used to be frowned on, but as life moves faster and faster, it's becoming more and more acceptable. Always send an individual cover letter, though, never a photocopied one. If you're lucky enough to get more than one offer, take them at once to an agent – if a publisher is interested then the agent will be, too.

Whichever method you try:

~ Approach the publisher in the way they prefer; consult the reference books or ring the editorial office and ask.

~ Get the name of the appropriate editor and address your package to them *by name.*

~ Enclose adequate return postage.

When you're offered a contract, ask the Society of Authors (page 16) to vet it for you; the offer of a book contract makes you eligible to apply for membership.

You could ask your editor to recommend

an agent. Certainly, do this if you don't feel confident about handling the business side of the deal yourself.

Publishing opportunities are opening up on the Internet all the time. *

If this option interests you, consult the reference books for the names of established Internet publishers. They usually operate by making material available for downloading in return for a fee from the buyer. The author gets a percentage of every copy of their book sold. This might be as high as 50%, though the selling prices are much lower than for conventional books.

There are also companies offering to showcase work that's looking for a publisher, but be wary of paying high fees for this kind of service. Few publishers bother to trawl the virtual world looking for writers – they have plenty of hard-copy manuscripts to keep them busy.

* It's new, it's big, and it's here to stay. Treat it with some caution, though – there are plenty of sharks out there.

Helping to sell your novel

Help your publisher promote and sell your novel: *

~ Take a copy to your local bookshop manager and suggest a 'local author' display and/or a signing session.

~ Take copies to your local newspaper office and radio station; offer to write a piece for them or do an interview to coincide with publication.

~ Ask friends to post reviews on Internet bookshop sites.

~ Liaise closely with your publisher's publicity team, making yourself available for any promotional events they organise and giving them plenty of notice of any other events you're asked to take part in.

~ Create your own website, and ask friends to mention your book on their websites.

Your publisher has many other books to promote. You are totally focused on your book, so do everything you can to help it sell.

Summary points

★ Write a novel that's saleable in today's market-place.

★ Revise, rewrite and polish your novel till it's as good as you can possibly make it.

★ Prepare a submission package that will impress agents and publishers.

★ Find the right agent for your novel and approach them in a businesslike way.

★ Offer your novel directly to publishers, if you can't find an agent or if you want to try multiple submissions.

★ Help your publisher to sell your novel by being available for interviews and book signings.

4 Getting Your Poetry Published

*'The essence of poetry is invention; such invention as,
by producing something unexpected, surprises and delights.'*
(Samuel Johnson)

In this chapter, five things that really matter:

~ **Keeping up to date**
~ **Getting started with the small press**
~ **Entering poetry competitions**
~ **Building a collection**
~ **Publishing your own poetry**

Writing poetry is something you do for love, not money. Very few magazines pay for poetry, and while you might win a few poetry prizes, you're hardly likely to get rich.

In spite of that, competition for publication is fierce. A well-established poetry magazine might receive 50,000 submissions a year, and only have space to publish a few hundred.

So how can you maximise your chances?

Accept that there's a lot more to writing poetry than simply setting words out in lines on paper. Poetry is a craft as well as an art; it demands that you combine essential elements to communicate the emotion you want to share with your readers. Be prepared to learn the craft.

Is this you?

I would like to get my poetry published but have no idea how to go about it. • Editors don't seem to be interested in the kind of poetry I write. • Why does nobody pay for poetry? • I've had a few poems published and I would now like to see a collection of my poems in print, but I don't know where to start. • Aren't poetry competitions a bit of a rip-off?

Keeping up to date

Read and study the poetry that is being published today. If you're out of touch with the current scene, you can't know what today's poetry editors want.

Many aspiring poets display scant knowledge of anything written in the last half-century, let alone in recent years. Too much poetry submitted to magazines is hopelessly archaic in language and style.

Read, read, read, and be open to what is happening *now*. Editors don't necessarily want wildly experimental or 'modern' forms, but they do expect poets to use the language and imagery of our world today.

Poetry editors despair at the poor craftsmanship shown by many aspiring poets. Study how poetry works: how sound, rhythm, rhyming patterns and form combine to convey not only meaning but emotion too.

Good contemporary poetry takes many forms.

Getting started with the small press

We should value our small press. These independent magazines keep poetry publishing alive. They can publish what they choose, whether it's traditional or avant-garde, because they don't have to answer to the accountant-led world of commercial publishing. Don't waste your time sending poetry to publishing houses; very few publish poetry, and none will want to know you unless you're famous. *

A few independent presses receive Arts Council grants, and some sell in bookshops, but most have to rely on subscriptions. Their publications are produced on tiny budgets and depend on reciprocal advertising with other independents.

Some small-press magazines pay for contributions, but most can only afford to give you a free copy or two of the issue in which your poetry appears. The situation could be different, though: if everyone who writes poetry subscribed to one magazine or bought just one volume of poetry a year, poetry would be the biggest branch of publishing. Sadly, far more people write poetry than read it.

* Collections of poetry sell poorly anyway; even established poets do well to sell in the low hundreds of copies.

Find the magazines you like and support them. Each has its own distinctive flavour, and some will suit you more than others. Look at a variety – most editors will send a single issue for the cover price plus postage – and when you find one you like and which you feel is in tune with your poetry, take out a subscription. You need to familiarise yourself with the editor's likes and dislikes; you need to be sure, too, that you're happy with the company your poetry would be keeping. *

Don't ask for free copies 'to study your magazine' or 'to see if I like it'. Very few independents make a profit; don't expect them to subsidise your market study or postage costs. Why should they?

Never send anything without an s.a.e. – it will probably go straight into the bin.

It's in your own interest to help keep poetry publishing alive. You need these magazines as much as they need you.

When you've got to know the editor's likes and dislikes, submit some of your work, set

* *Don't submit poetry to any publication you wouldn't be proud to see your name in.*

out in the standard form as shown on page 96, one poem per A4 page, with your name and address on every page.

Don't send more than six poems at once, and don't forget the s.a.e.

You'll save time, money and aggravation all round if you:

~ Don't submit your poetry to big publishers – yet.

~ Don't send poetry to magazines that never publish it; they won't make exceptions, however good you are.

~ Do suit your submissions to your target magazine: don't send an epic to a pocket-sized publication.

~ *Never* send the same poem to more than one editor at a time. *

~ Do keep records of what you send where.

A few mainstream magazines and some newspapers publish poetry. There are also markets for greeting card verse. Check out the yearbooks.

* *The poetry world is small, and someone is sure to notice (and complain to the editors) if your poem appears in two magazines at the same time.*

Entering poetry competitions

Big poetry competitions are more like lotteries than contests. A competition offering big prizes attracts thousands of entries; don't imagine that a single judge, or each member of a panel of judges, reads every entry. Where there is one judge, the organisers usually sift the entries down to the number the 'name' judge has agreed to look at. Where there is more than one judge, the entries are usually split equally among them, each judge compiling a short-list of poems which are then read by all the judges. This is where the gamble comes in: a judge who might have liked and short-listed your poem might never even see it.

Don't let this put you off entering, though. Most competitions are run fairly, and ask for anonymous entries, so your poem has as much chance as one entered by a famous poet.

There's a huge amount of prestige attached to winning a big national or international competition, so it's worth having a go. You could have a better chance, though, and maybe get some feedback, with competitions organised by independent magazines.

A word about entry fees: some competitions ask for fees which are out of proportion to the prize-money offered. You might not think it worth entering a competition which, for example, asks for an entry fee of £3 or £4 but offers a top prize of only £50. A fairer deal might be a £3 fee for a top prize of £250 or £300.

Keep in mind what most judges look for:

~ individual vision and imagination

~ tone and language appropriate to the poem's subject

~ genuine feeling and communication

~ craftsmanship.

And to give your entry at least a chance, check that

~ you've read *all* the rules and followed them absolutely

~ you've understood and followed any special instructions

~ you've enclosed the correct entry fee

~ you've kept a copy of your work.

A caution: sometimes competitions are advertised that invite poets to submit work free of submission fees and promising publication of the winning poems in an anthology. These anthologies are then offered to participating poets, usually at high prices, and often with extra incentives to buy, perhaps promising that your poem will be specially showcased.

There is nothing illegal in this, but if you value your reputation as a poet you should avoid these competitions. No poem is ever rejected, and your poem might appear alongside very poor quality verse; the 'judges' offer praise indiscriminately and will include any poem, regardless of merit, for the sole purpose of parting poets from their money. *

I've tested this myself (as have other writers) by submitting rubbish 'poetry' which was lavishly praised and awarded 'semi-finalist' status.

Building a collection

When you've had a substantial number of poems published in reputable magazines, think about putting a collection together. You can include new poems alongside published work, if you wish. The important thing is that you'll be presenting yourself to a publisher as an established poet with a respectable track record.

It's courteous to acknowledge previous publication by naming the relevant magazines.

Publishing your own poetry

There's no reason at all why you shouldn't publish your own poetry. You could either publish a volume of your collected poetry, or have your poems printed individually, perhaps as greeting cards. *

Don't be flattered into paying good money to the ever-predatory 'vanity' publisher, who will charge large sums for what is seldom more than a printing service.

Many poets sell self-published poetry booklets and greeting cards to raise funds for charity.

Your local printer should be able to do at least as good a job. They'll give you an even better deal if you give them 'camera-ready copy': set out your poems on your computer exactly as you want them to appear and print them out in clear black ink. This saves typesetting costs.

Summary points

★ Keep up to date. Read the poetry that is being published today.

★ Getting started with the small press will get your foot on the publishing ladder.

★ Enter poetry competitions, particularly those that offer publication.

★ Building a substantial body of published work will enable you to offer a collection to a publisher.

★ Publishing your own poetry is a perfectly acceptable way of getting your work into print.

5 Writing and Selling Short Non-Fiction

'The two most beautiful words in the English language are "Check enclosed".'
                                    (Dorothy Parker)

In this chapter, five things that really matter:

~ **Getting to know the markets**
~ **Starting small with fillers**
~ **Moving on to articles and features**
~ **Selling with a great query letter**
~ **Getting yourself known as a specialist**

Factual pieces of all kinds are in far greater demand than short stories. They're not necessarily easier to write, but they're certainly a lot easier to sell. Nearly all magazine articles are supplied by freelance writers – writers like us.

Every writer – and that includes you – has some knowledge and experience that would interest, entertain, amuse, or help other people. And whatever your ultimate writing ambition might be, short non-fiction is the quickest way to get started. A record of published work will boost your confidence and open doors.

Every successful writer keeps abreast of what's currently in demand. Look for possible markets on the news-stands, in writers' magazines and yearbooks, in trade and company directories … there are opportunities everywhere.

Is this you?

I'm a beginning writer and don't know where to start. • I want to write articles but don't know which subjects would sell best. • I've read advice that says I should write about what I know, but this seems a bit limiting to me. • I've written an article I believe would help other people but don't know where to sell it. • I've been advised to study the market but I'm not really sure how to do this. • How do I know what to say to editors – I've never met any?

Getting to know the markets

The key to success is knowing where and how to sell what you want to write.

Before you approach any publication, check that it's willing to consider freelance material. Get guidelines if they're available.

Use only current issues for market study. Back issues might be cheaper, but might give you out-of-date information. Check the publication's content, style and language so you can offer the right kind of material written in the appropriate style: *

Content

Your idea will be rejected if your subject matter is alien to your target publication's area of interest. *Hello!* won't be interested in a report on your village swimming gala; *Amateur Photography*'s readers don't want to read advice on caring for cats.

Style

Is the writing formal, with dense prose and longish paragraphs – or more casual, with

* *Do your homework thoroughly, and only send material editors can use.*

punchy paragraphs and perhaps using bullet points for emphasis?

Language

Are the words short and simple, or sophisticated and multi-syllabic? Are the sentences short and straightforward, or more complex, with subordinate clauses? Are the words used and the overall tone, for the most part, colloquial or formal?

Build a picture of the publication's typical reader – the ads will help you here – and keep that person in mind while you put your query together. *

When you eventually write your piece, write as if you're talking to this person.

Remember the pictures; having photographs to offer could help your sale. Ideally, use two cameras, one for transparencies (slides) and one for prints. If you can only take one camera use transparency film – prints can be made from transparencies but not vice versa. Don't use

An effective query letter will convince the editor your idea is worth considering, and that you know how to handle it.

digital cameras – yet. Digital photos don't yet enlarge well enough for reproduction in quality magazines.

Don't send originals until you're asked to, send photocopies. Sending photos the editor hasn't asked for is unprofessional.

Remember what the readership – and the editor – expect.

Starting small with fillers

A filler is a short item that used to be put in to fill up the end of a column in a newspaper or magazine, to avoid leaving blank space. Nowadays, fillers are popular pieces in their own right. Editors like them because they know their readers enjoy intriguing or amusing little items.

Fillers can range from pithy phrases to 300- to 400-word mini-articles: household hints, money- or time-saving tips, recipes, epigrams, jokes, puzzles, quips, daft definitions, fascinating facts, mottoes, children's amusing comments, anecdotes, typographical errors, light verse, 'on this day' historical notes or nostalgic memories … are you reaching for pen and paper already? *

'Readers' letters' also come into the 'filler' category; almost every magazine uses these, and some pay substantial cash or prize rewards for them.

You can send several fillers at a time to the same magazine, but don't send the same filler to more than one magazine at a time.

It isn't customary to send an s.a.e. with fillers, unless you're sending photographs you want returned. If you haven't heard from the editor in about six months, you can assume your material isn't going to be used and it's safe to submit it to the next market on your list. Keep copies, and keep a note of where you've sent every filler.

Keep a notebook with you all the time and jot down any ideas that strike you – don't risk forgetting them.

The scope for filler material is as wide as your imagination.

Moving on to articles and features

Most magazine editors are happy to consider

work from new writers provided what you offer is appropriate to their publication. Editors despair that so many would-be contributors don't read their magazines; they get tired of ploughing through piles of totally unsuitable submissions. This is a major reason why so many magazines won't consider unsolicited submissions. Lazy, careless writers make things unnecessarily difficult for the rest of us.

Whatever type of article you're writing, keep careful notes of your sources. Some publications (*Reader's Digest*, for example) check them out meticulously.

New writers are often advised to 'write about what you know'. That's sound advice to a degree, but it can be a lot more stimulating to write about topics that fire your imagination. There are plenty of ways to research these, and your enthusiasm will shine through your writing and make it even more saleable.

The following are the most saleable article types – as you can see, there's something for everyone:

~ **Personality pieces**: profiles, interviews, news about famous people; these are top of the 'wanted' list.

~ **How to**: showing how to do or make something, how to save time or money.

~ **Self-help**: a type of 'how to', giving advice, guidance and encouragement in areas of human psychology and behaviour.

~ **Personal experience**: relating a first-hand experience, written in the first person (possibly as an '… as told to …' piece).

~ **Inspirational** (sometimes called a 'brightener'): aiming to inspire hope and courage in its readers, often with a 'triumph over tragedy' slant.

~ **Service**: usually aimed at the consumer, giving a range of product choices, possibly including advice on selection and value for money.

~ **'Round-up' or survey**: comments, opinions, information, advice, quotes, etc. on any topic, gathered from experts, celebrities, the person-in-the-street …

~ **Essay, commentary, opinion**: a personal opinion or exploration of a subject or issue.

~ **Profile**: a word-portrait of a person (or possibly an animal).

~ **Historical**: focusing on people, places and events in history.

~ **Nostalgia**: looking fondly at the past, usually with a personal and positive focus, appealing to readers' sentiments and emotions. Usually has a strong 'those were the days …' flavour.

~ **Anniversary**: recalling, re-examining, or enlarging on a past event. Subjects can range from the famous to the local or the long-forgotten, and are featured in newspapers and magazines on or near the date of the event's anniversary.

~ **Investigative/exposé**: reporting researched and documented information about an important, possibly controversial, subject.

~ **Travel**: people and places, customs and cultures, in the UK and worldwide.

~ **Humour**: An article written specifically to amuse, as distinct from a 'straight' article written with a touch of humour. Often written in the first person. (Humorous material is the only kind you can't sell with a query. The editor needs to see the whole piece.)

Selling with a great query letter

A query letter is a letter you write to a specific editor to get him or her interested in the article or feature you hope they'll want to buy and publish. *

You pitch your idea so the editor can see that

~ your topic will interest their readers

~ you know your subject and will deal with it from a specific and appropriate angle

~ you can write clearly and concisely

* Persevere. Editors change; editorial tastes change. Too many beginning writers give up too easily and too soon.

~ you can supply supporting fact-boxes and leads to further information if required

~ you can supply relevant photographs if appropriate

~ you're totally familiar (and comfortable) with the magazine's style and ethos.

If you've already had articles published, enclose two or three photocopies with your query. This is not mandatory, but it will show the editor that someone else has considered your work good enough to publish.

Make your query strong and interesting, not bland and routine. For example, if you've interviewed an author whose novels go straight to the top of the bestseller lists and you're querying the editor of a glossy women's magazine, rather than writing 'Dear Angela Masthead, Would you be interested in' you could open your query with 'Dear Angela Masthead, On her dressing-table in her permanent suite at the Ritz, bestselling author Penny Dreadful keeps a photograph of a smiling, grey-haired woman pictured in the doorway of a tiny terraced cottage. "My grandmother," Penny says, touching the photo affectionately. "I look at her every morning. I never want to forget where I came from." '

When the editor asks to see the complete piece, make sure it does everything you promised in your query letter. *

Don't change your mind about the subject matter, the angle or the treatment. If you let any editor down in this way, they'll be reluctant to look at anything else you might offer.

Getting yourself known as a specialist

It's great fun to be a generalist writer, covering anything that takes your interest. It's a lot more profitable, though, to concentrate on one or two specific areas of interest and get yourself known as a specialist.

Editors have confidence in a writer whose record demonstrates a wide and thorough

* *Be professional. Deliver what you promised; you want to make your mark as a reliable contributor.*

knowledge of their subject. By concentrating on a specific field of interest, you'll build a reputation as someone editors can turn to when they need material in that field. Find your niche and editors will be ringing you. You'd like to be in that position, wouldn't you? It's what every writer wants.

Specialisation has another advantage: with a substantial amount of published work to your credit, you could write a book on your subject. Your track record as a specialist will give you a strong chance of having a book accepted for publication.

Summary points

★ Increase your success rate by getting to know and understand the market.

★ Start small by writing fillers.

★ Move on to longer articles and features.

★ Sell your work the professional way, with a great query letter.

★ Find your niche and get yourself known as a specialist.

6 Writing and Publishing a Non-Fiction Book

'A writer's material is what he cares about.'
(John Gardner)

In this chapter, six things that really matter:

~ **Assessing your idea: will it make a book?**

~ **Preparing your sales package**

~ **First find your publisher**

~ **Approaching a publisher**

~ **Delivering your manuscript – on time**

~ **Helping to promote your book**

Here are a couple of statistics for you to think about: of the 100,000 or so books published every year in the UK, non-fiction outnumbers fiction by ten to one; yet there are at least ten times more aspiring novelists than non-fiction writers.

The first-time non-fiction writer, then, is at least ten times more likely to succeed than the first-time novelist.

Your chances will be even better if you take the professional writer's approach to getting published: know your subject, prepare a sales package, find a publisher and secure a contract *before* you write your book.

A caution: Unless you're already famous, or have done something truly amazing and newsworthy, *don't write your memoirs*. The only companies who will publish the person-in-the-street's life story are 'vanity' publishers. Dealing with these companies could cost you dearly. Read and heed the warnings in the reference books (page 16).

Is this you?

I've read that everyone has at least one book inside them, but I'm not sure that's true. • I've got an idea for a book, but that's as far as I've got. • There are quite a lot of books already in print on the subject I'm thinking of writing about – should I bother? • I'm writing a book, but I've run out of steam after a couple of chapters. • I'm writing a book and I'd like to know how to get it published when it's finished. • I've written a book on my pet subject, but I can't afford to keep making new copies to send to publishers; is there a better way to sell it?

Assessing your idea: will it make a book?

Writing a full-length book is hard work. Before you commit yourself, you need to be sure your idea is strong enough to make a book. Ask yourself:

~ Is this subject big enough to fill a whole book, without waffle or padding? *An A-to-Z of Garden Maintenance* would be; *How to Mow Your Lawn* would not – it would only make an article.

~ Do you know enough about the topic to write an interesting, informative and fact-packed book about it?

~ Can you convince a publisher that you are the right person to write this book? The more credentials you can offer the better.

For example, if you want to write a book on running a successful business from home, your chances will be infinitely greater if you have actually run a successful home business. Your hands-on experience will be a strong selling point.

Your credentials might include:

~ education, diplomas and degrees attained, lectures given

~ business or job experience

~ life experience

~ publication of articles or papers on your subject

~ membership of professional or trade organisations

~ awards won.

Would enough people want to buy your book to make it commercially viable? Publishers are in business to make money; they look for books that will appeal to a wide readership and sell a healthy number of copies. *

If you're writing a book on a specialised subject, perhaps with a limited market, you might need a specialist publisher.

Preparing your sales package

You're asking a publisher to invest in your book. Your sales package must persuade them they won't be wasting their time or money. You need to prepare a detailed presentation of the book you want them to buy, aiming to produce a proposal they won't be able to resist. Include

~ a concise overview of your book

~ what market you envisage for it – that is, who will buy it

~ an assessment of competitive titles already on the market

~ how *your* book will be different and better

~ your credentials as the right person to write this book

* You must convince the publisher your book will make money for them, or they won't be interested.

~ a chapter-by-chapter outline of the whole book

~ one or two sample chapters; put your best work into these – the editor needs to see that you can write well. *

First find your publisher

Don't write your book before you have a contract from a publisher. There's no point in completing the whole project when your publisher might ask you to approach your subject from a different angle, or tailor it to fit a series.

Study the book publishers listed in the reference books. Flag those currently publishing the type of book you're writing, and list those that look most likely. Go to bookshops and note any likely publishers not already on your list. Ask writer friends to recommend publishers.

From your list of possible publishers, choose the most promising and get catalogues: write to, or phone, the publicity departments, or look on the Internet.

* Publishing is a buyer's market; make this sample the very best you can do.

Find out which editor at your first-choice publisher handles the kind of book you want to offer – phone the switchboard and ask; your proposal must reach the right person. Get the spelling right. *

The reference books might help, but check anyway, as editors move around a lot.

Don't try to discuss your book on the phone, unless you're asked to; the reference books usually specify the publisher's preferred method of approach – some might be happy to talk on the phone, but most prefer a written proposal they can take time to assess.

Avoid publishers who have recently released a book on your topic – they're unlikely to want another.

If you have any contact with a suitable publisher (you might have met one at a writers' conference or been introduced by a friend), send them an exclusive submission. If you have no 'in' anywhere, you could try sending your proposal to several publishers at once, to save time.

* You don't like it when people get your name wrong, do you? Why risk getting off to a bad start?

Approaching a publisher

Remember that it's essential to write to an editor or publisher *by name*. Anything sent to 'The Publishing Company' or to 'The Editor' could hang around for months.

Write a letter to each of your first three short-listed editors, briefly describing your book in a paragraph or two, and offering to send a proposal if the editor would like to see one. If you hear nothing after about a month, write a brief follow-up note, or phone or email the editor to ask if your letter was received. Remind the editor of the title of your book and (briefly) its subject, and ask if they would like to see your proposal.

If you don't get a nibble of interest, try the next three names on your list, checking first that your named editors haven't moved on.

Be professional at all times. Editors have to deal every day with letters, emails, phone calls, proposals and manuscripts. Respect their time. Accept the hard fact that you need them more than they need you. Behave like a professional and you'll at least have a chance of being treated like one.

Don't give up. More would-be writers have failed through lack of persistence than lack of ability.

Be open to criticism and advice. If editors who reject your proposal offer comments, think about them. If several editors offer similar comments, perhaps pointing out areas of weakness, their suggestions might be valid. *

When a publisher does offer you a contract, remember that you can approach the Society of Authors (page 16) for advice before you sign anything.

Delivering your manuscript – on time

You've agreed terms with your publisher and signed your contract. Now all you have to do is write the book.

Your editor might ask for changes to your original outline; she might ask you to alter the running order of your chapters, change the handling of some aspects of your topic,

* Publishing is about marketing, not about writers or writing. Publishers (usually) know what will sell and what won't.

add sections or delete others.

Look at any suggestions with an open mind. If you are strongly against particular changes, be clear about your reasons for resisting them, so you can present a sound argument if you feel you must. Do your best to keep things on an amicable footing, though. Remember you're both on the same side – you both want the book to be a success. *

You might want to make changes to your original outline yourself. Generally, your editor won't object to this – an outline is just an outline, after all, not a declaration chiselled in stone. There is seldom any need to discuss small changes here and there, but you should discuss anything major.

Most editors are reasonably flexible, but remember that, while you might know more about your subject, your editor has more experience in producing successful books. It's in your best interest to work amicably with the editor to make your book as good as possible.

* *Don't get a reputation for being difficult to deal with. You might want to do business with this editor again in the future.*

And don't forget the 'acceptable manuscript' clause in your contract (it's always there) giving the publisher power to reject your manuscript outright, without compensation, if they consider it unacceptable.

If you need guidance on putting together a publishable non-fiction book, there are many excellent manuals available.

Make your book reader-friendly. Don't strive for a style that doesn't come naturally to you. Use plain language and simple sentence structures that convey your information clearly to your reader. Aim to 'talk on paper'.

Edit and prune your manuscript before you send it in. Get rid of any padding, any superfluous words; you'll strengthen your writing by being concise. Be meticulous about correcting errors of spelling and grammar.

Prepare your manuscript in the accepted prose format (see page 95), and deliver it by the agreed date. *

* If you deliver your manuscript late without prior arrangement, you risk holding up the entire publishing schedule.

If you're not going to meet the deadline *for any reason*, ask for an extension as soon as you know you'll need it – don't leave it till the last minute.

If your publisher requires the work on disk as well as hard (paper) copy, use the format requested. Don't forget to keep a complete hard copy of the finished work as well as an electronic copy – you might have to consult it quickly if your editor phones with a query.

Helping to promote your book

Your publisher's publicity team will probably send you an Author Questionnaire. Give this plenty of thought. It will ask for information about yourself and your book.

Much of this information is already in your proposal, but the publicity team might not see that. In your own interest, take time to fill in the questionnaire as completely as possible. You want the publicity for your book to be as dynamic as the team can make it. *

* Books don't sell themselves. Everyone concerned has to work hard to get a book noticed – and that includes the author.

Be ready to cooperate when you're asked to do press or radio interviews or bookshop signings. If you're lucky, you might even get a chance to promote your book on television. Respond with a smile to whatever you're asked to do, even if it means getting up at dawn to get to a radio station.

If you come up with a good idea yourself, pitch it to the publicity team. Don't push it, though, if they're unwilling, and don't go ahead on your own without their agreement. It's their responsibility, their budget and their right to decide what's appropriate.

Of course, you can promote your book locally and at writers' events. It's courteous, though, to keep the team informed.

There are few things more satisfying than publishing a book that attracts notice – and good reviews. And your book might change someone's life. They might even write and tell you so.

Summary points

★ Assess your idea – it must be strong enough to make a book.

★ Prepare a proposal editors will find irresistible.

★ Find your publisher before you write your book.

★ Make the right approach to the right publisher.

★ Deliver a great manuscript.

★ Help the publicity team to promote your book.

Example of a standard prose layout.
Published in *My Weekly* (UK) and *Woman's Day* (Australia)

Short story: 'What About Emma?'   Chriss McCallum
1,900 words   Any House
                                         Any Street
                                         Anywhere
                                         AN1 1NY
                                         Tel: 0100 011 0111

What About Emma?

by Chriss McCallum

Martin concluded: 'So I'll be based in the States for at least
two years. Will you come with me, Julia? Marry me?'

   Carefully, Julia lowered her coffee cup on to its saucer.
She should have been ready for this. The signals had all
been there. The unexpected invitation to lunch. Their
favourite table in their favourite restaurant. The single
perfect rose. The excitement in Martin's voice as he talked
about the new project, the opportunities, the need for total
involvement …

                                                    mf

Example of how to set out a poem.
Published in *Reach* magazine.

The Poet's Voice

The poet, searching for his voice,
might try the tones of Yeats or Joyce,
might practise in the Eliot style
with sly allusion, subtle smile,
might look to Larkin's candid muse
or probe the power of lusty Hughes.

But when it's time to make a choice
the poet, searching for his voice,
won't find it with that lofty throng,
but in his own heart's honest song.

Chriss McCallum

Chriss McCallum
Any House
Any Street
Anywhere
AN1 1NY
Tel: 0100 011 0111